CHIMNEY BOOK

Tim Battle

IDEA EDITIONS

I gratefully acknowledge the following
for their considerable help and encouragement:
The Department of the Environment, The National Trust,
The Crown Estates, The National Coal Board
and all those who pot spotted for me
and whose examples may, or may not, be included.
Tim Battle.

Text and photographs Towco Holdings Ltd. © 1977
Typography and book design by Roy Walker, MSIA
Originally published by Idea E, s.r.l., Via Cappuccio 21,
20123 Milan, Italy. October 1977
ISBN 0 905093 00 4

Distributed internationally by Idea Books Distribution,
Paris, Milan, London, Amsterdam and Sydney.

Printed in Italy by G. Spinelli & C. S.p.A., Florence.

Photolito: Zincografica Felsinea s.n.c. - Bologna

Chimneys, with their pots, on first inspection come in a variety of odd sizes and shapes, ancient and modern, elegant and ungainly. Their only obvious common factor is that they are designed to lift smoke from a fire.

It is only when one looks up and observes them in relationship to their surroundings, or as an essential architectural detail helping to make up the whole, that their importance is fully appreciated. Their soaring elegance or squat outline provides a natural focal point for the eye to touch upon; tree tops and chimneys blending together to give an immediate indenti-kit of home when viewed from afar. The Chimney Book is a personal anthology of satisfying images and shapes. It seeks to hint at, to suggest to the inquisitive eye, the enormous selection spawned on a National, cultural, historical or simply decorative basis.

Chimneys originated in the 13th Century, one of the earliest surviving working examples in Britain being that at the Abbey Buildings, Abingdon, Berkshire. In about 1630-1640 coal began to replace scarce wood as the main domestic fuel, which in turn demanded higher and more efficient chimneys to carry away the denser and hotter gases. Hence the splendid variety and range of Tudor chimneys, a superb opportunity for imaginative architects and master builders alike to display their skills.

In 1880 a Count Romford devised a set of rules for the design of domestic fireplaces and chimneys which significantly improved the performance of the open hearth fire.

The great volume of building that was generated in the 19th Century by the Industrial Revolution not only threw up superb examples of mill and mine chimneys, but also gave row upon row of terraced houses, each with their own cluster of pots contributing to the haze of smoke that used to loom over large cities on a still autumn evening before the arrival of smokeless fuel.

Chimney pots and cowls are opportunities for self-expression and choice by each new householder, a visible witness to local customs in beating the prevailing winds, of overcoming downdraughts or unwitting sexual symbolism.

It is in Portugal, on the Algarve, where the use of chimneys as a decorative medium has become a splendid art form. Colourful exotica floating high above the rooftops in the hot sunshine give exciting chimneys for all to admire, not to use!

In complete contrast to the Algarve are Europe's grey, mass, housing estates of urban man, where the value of an amenity in financial terms is so finely judged that it has been decided that the cost of a chimney, and the accompanying warm focal point of the family fireplace, is too high. This negative attitude to the chimney and the open hearth is surely one of passing fashion, and we will continue again to produce fine examples of this expressive form for future generations to admire.

1

11 | 12
13 | 14

21 | 22